# Izzy the Interjection

Written by Coert Voorhees
Illustrations by Powerhouse Animation

# Meet the Parts of Speech

I name a specific person, place, thing, or idea. It's a big responsibility, naming things—a responsibility that requires a certain attention to detail.

Vinny the Action Verb

Some people say I'm all over the place. Some people call me a ball of energy. I take that as a compliment, because I just like to go, go, go!

I take the place of one or more Nouns or Pronouns. I always want the Noun's job, and I hang out with the Verb and Adjective.

Lucy the Linking Verb

I'm perfectly happy to link Nouns and Pronouns with the appropriate Adjectives, but it's not like I'm going to expend a lot of energy doing so.

I modify a Noun or Pronoun. I tell what kind, which one, how many, or how much. I pride myself on being the most artistic of the parts of speech.

Connie the Conjunction

Gather 'round everybody and let's have ourselves a wonderful time. I just love bringing words and groups of words together, don't you?

I modify a Verb, Adjective, or other Adverb. I tell how, when, where, to what extent, and under what condition. I often end in –ly, but I don't have to.

Izzy the Interjection

I express emotion!! Yep, I'm always here, always ready with my commas and exclamation points, just in case.

They call me Preposition because I'm pre-positioned. I'm first. At the front. Before every other word in the phrase? Got it?

Slang

I am a chameleon. A spy. An undercover operative. I infiltrate the sentence and act as whatever part of speech suits me.

IZZY THE INTERJECTION



Graphic Design by Mckee Frazior
Printed by Friesens, Altona, Manitoba, Canada



This book is typeset in Komika Text

Distributed throughout the world by Ingram Publisher Services www.ingrambook.com

Printed in Canada

Izzy the interjection expressed emotion.

Bravo!

Yowee!

Golly!

Oh, what a morning!

She expressed moderate emotion with a comma.
Hmmm, what should I have for breakfast?
CRUNCHY FLAKES
milk

She expressed strong emotion with an exclamation mark.

She spent every day searching for ways to express emotion.
Bye, Mom.
Goodbye!

Hi, Connie!
Have a fun and happy day.
Okay!

There were so many places for Izzy to express emotion.
GRAMMAROPOLIS CAFE
Grocery
Store
Gee, I wonder where to start.

She spent some time with Jake and his new a puppy.

She helped out when Li'l Pete finally understood advanced propulsion techniques.
Now my rocket will fly straight through the air.
Eureka!

And she was the first on the scene when Roger saw the day's lottery numbers.
I did it! I picked them all!
Yippee! Hooray!
TODAY'S WINNING LOTTERY NUMBERS:
1, 8, 17, 19, 23, 26, 28, 37, 43, 45, 51, 56, 60, 63, 70, 72, 75

But her interjections weren't always positive.
I didn't pick them all. I missed one.
LOTTERY TICKET
1, 8,
17, 19,
23, 26,
28, 37,
43, 45,
Arrggg! Shucks! Fiddlesticks!
NEWS
She was really good at expressing frustration and disappointment.

She was great at expressing pain.
My toe!
Ouch!
CONCRETE
CONCRETE

She expressed regret quite well.
Connie's Couture
Bad dog!
Alas!

From time to time, Izzy and her friend Slang even had interjection competitions.
Yay!
Sweet!
Drat!
Bummer.
Ha!
Rofl.

But because she wasn't grammatically related to the rest of the sentence, she was often lonely when there was no emotion to express.
Hello?
Um, where is everyone?

Hey, Nelson. How are you?
I'm fine.
Fine like "Meh" or fine like "Blah"?
Just fine.
BUS STOP

She just wanted a chance to express some emotion.
BUS
Oh, you dropped these.
Ahem!

So she sat down and waited for something to happen.

Until finally something *did* happen.

MOVE IT
Moving Company

Uh oh!

Izzy leapt to her feet and used a comma to express mild emotion.
Hey, Roger.
Yo, wake up.
Z
Z
Z
Z

Mild emotion wasn't enough, so she used an exclamation mark to express strong emotion.
Hey! Yo!
Dude!
ZZZZ

She hopped into the car, shoved Roger to the side, and slammed on the brakes.
Aaaahhh!

After that, there were plenty of interjections to go around.
Phew!
Wha?
Hooray!
Hooray!
Hooray!

Stop!
Do not read.

# INTERJECTIONS

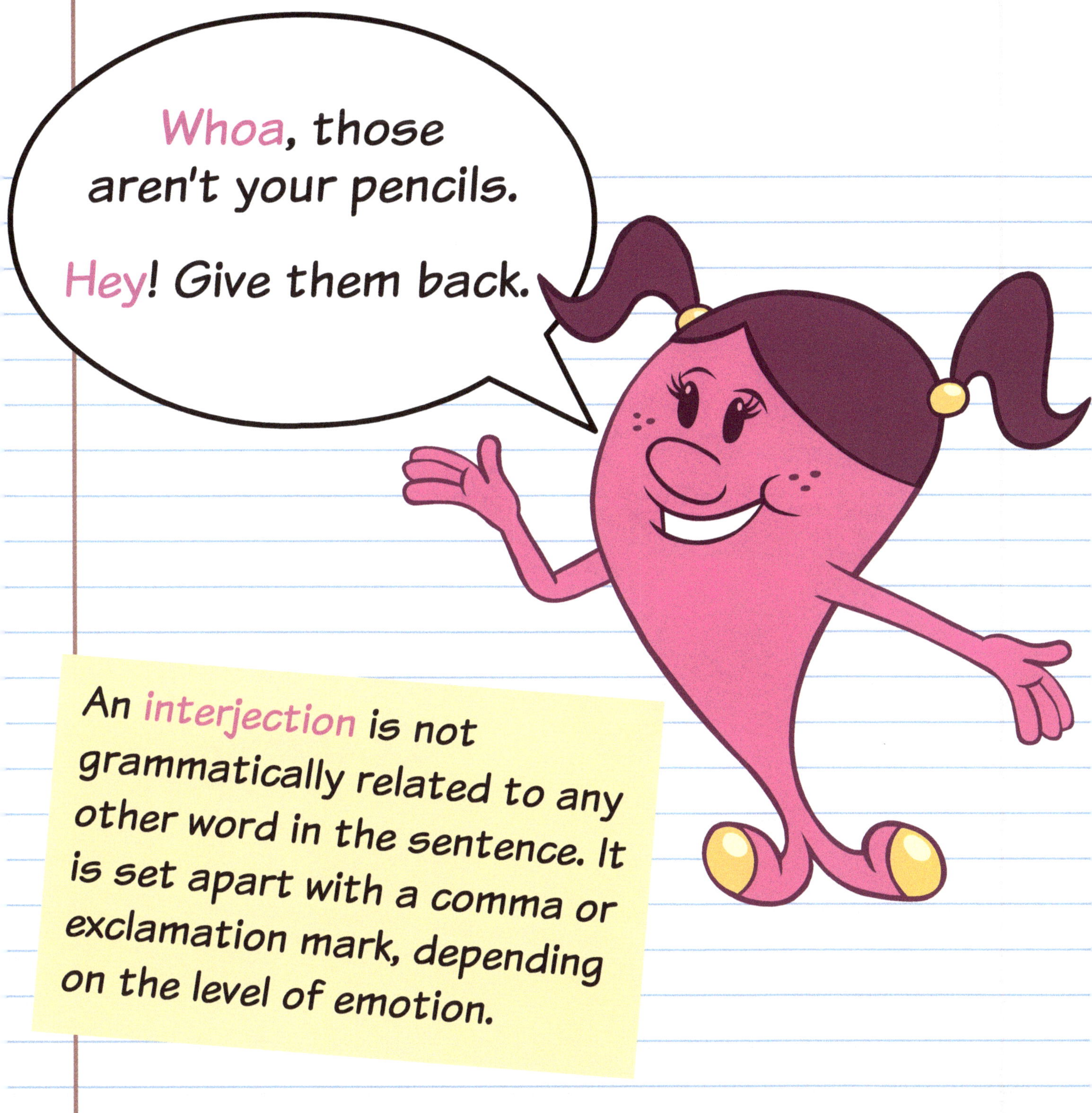
Whoa, those aren't your pencils.
Hey! Give them back.
An interjection is not grammatically related to any other word in the sentence. It is set apart with a comma or exclamation mark, depending on the level of emotion.

Mild emotion is set apart by a comma.

Wow, those potato chips sure were expensive.

Hey, stop looking at me like that.

Gee, your friends are nice.

Wow
Hey
Gee

# STRONG EMOTION

Strong emotion is set apart with an exclamation mark.

Yay! I just won the lottery!

Oh no! That guy just stole my winning lottery ticket!

Hooray! The police caught the guy who stole my winning lottery ticket!

## EXAMPLES

Yay
Oh no
Hooray

CPSIA information can be obtained
at www.ICGtesting.com
Printed in the USA
BVHW050946120519
547997BV00003B/8

9 781644 420126